## Natural Disasters

# Vibrating Volcanoes

### Julie Richards

This edition first published in 2002 in the United States of America by Chelsea House Publishers, a subsidiary of Haights Cross Communications.

Chelsea House Publishers
1974 Sproul Road, Suite 400
Broomall, PA 19008-0914

The Chelsea House world wide web address is www.chelseahouse.com

Library of Congress Cataloging-in-Publication Data Applied for.

ISBN 0-7910-6581-2

First published in 2001 by
Macmillan Education Australia Pty Ltd
627 Chapel Street, South Yarra, Australia 3141

Edited by Sally Woollett
Text design by Polar Design Pty Ltd
Cover design by Polár Design Pty Ltd
Illustrations and maps by Pat Kermode, Purple Rabbit Productions
Printed in Hong Kong

**Acknowledgements**
The author and the publisher are grateful to the following for permission to reproduce copyright material:

Cover photograph: Steam and ash bursting from volcanic eruption, courtesy of Photolibrary.com.

Andy Belcher/Legend Photography,  p. 19; Australian Picture Library/CORBIS, pp. 2, 3, 13, 14, 16, 18, 20, 22, 23, 24–25, 25 (right), 27, 28, 31, 32; Australian Picture Library/ZEFA, p. 10 (middle); NASA, p. 7; National Oceanic and Atmospheric Administration/Department of Commerce, pp. 15, 26; News Ltd., p. 17; PhotoDisc, pp. 5, 10 (bottom); Photolibrary.com, pp. 4, 8, 10 (top), 29.

# Contents

# Mountains of Fire

Did you know that rocks could **melt**?

Why is the Earth full of **holes**?

Did you know that there are mountains that can **spit fire** and blow thick **poisonous ash** so high into the sky that it changes the weather?

Perhaps you have heard of an **ancient** Italian city called **Pompeii**.

Pompeii was covered in so much ash and melted rock that it lay **buried** for over a thousand years.

What is it that can make all these things happen?
**A volcano!**

VOLCANOES can be dangerous to live near, although many people do so. They do this because volcanoes produce ash that is rich in minerals. These minerals help crops to grow strong and healthy.

When a volcano erupts it can do a lot of damage to the land around it. People can die from the poisonous smoke and burning **lava**. When something in nature harms people and destroys the places where they live, it is called a natural disaster.

# What is a volcano?

The Earth's **crust** is covered with cracks and holes. These cracks and holes are called volcanoes. Out of them pours something called **magma**. Magma looks very much like liquid fire, but it is really rock that has become so hot it has melted.

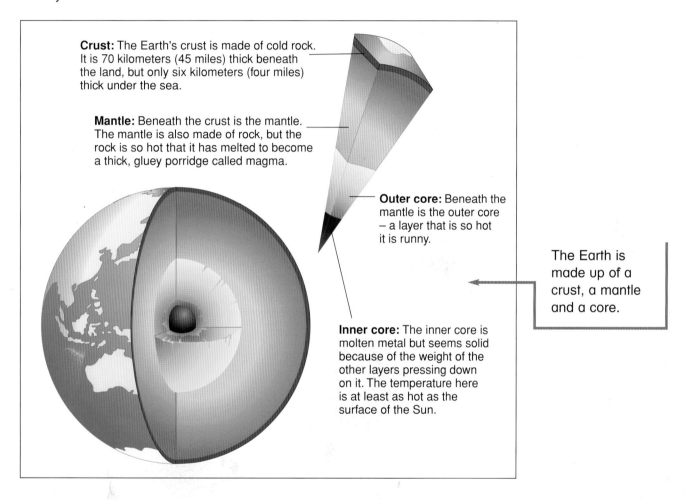

**Crust:** The Earth's crust is made of cold rock. It is 70 kilometers (45 miles) thick beneath the land, but only six kilometers (four miles) thick under the sea.

**Mantle:** Beneath the crust is the mantle. The mantle is also made of rock, but the rock is so hot that it has melted to become a thick, gluey porridge called magma.

**Outer core:** Beneath the mantle is the outer core – a layer that is so hot it is runny.

The Earth is made up of a crust, a mantle and a core.

**Inner core:** The inner core is molten metal but seems solid because of the weight of the other layers pressing down on it. The temperature here is at least as hot as the surface of the Sun.

## Making mountains from magma

Magma pushes its way up from deep inside the Earth. When it flows through the holes in the Earth's surface, it becomes lava. When lava cools it becomes solid rock. Slowly, the rock builds up layer by layer until it becomes a volcanic mountain. The top part of a volcano is called the **cone**. The bowl-shaped opening at the top of the cone is called the crater. Craters are caused by eruptions.

Disaster Detective

Lava can travel at 200 kilometers (120 miles) per hour, burning everything it touches. Can you find out what the temperature of lava is?

# Where are volcanoes found?

There are more than 1,500 active volcanoes in the world. Most of them are found close together along the edges of the Pacific Ocean. This group of volcanoes is known as the Ring of Fire. Why do so many volcanoes exist here? It has something to do with how the surface of the Earth is made.

The surface of the Earth is a thin layer of cold rock called the crust. Beneath the crust, a great river of magma is constantly moving. As it moves, the magma tugs at the Earth's crust, trying to pull it along. Magma is very hot; it can stretch and spread just like melted cheese, so it moves quite easily. However, the crust is too cold and hard to be as stretchy as magma. Instead of being dragged along in one piece, the Earth's crust has cracked and broken into several pieces.

The Earth's crust is broken up into pieces. Most volcanoes are found on or near the edges of these pieces.

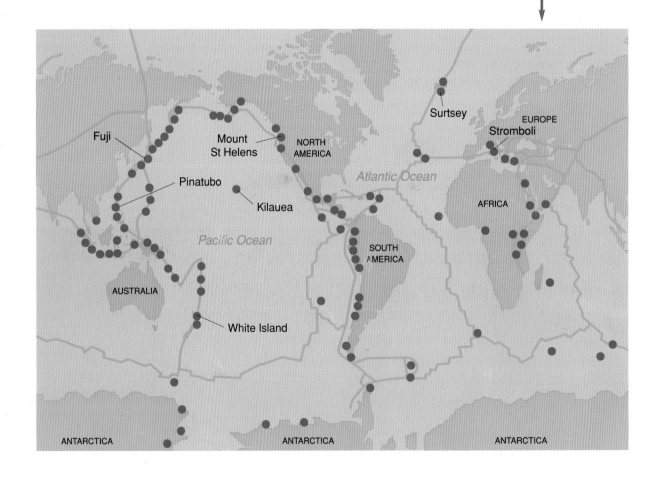

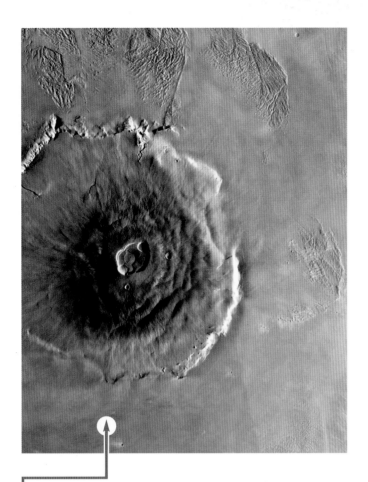

The largest known volcano, Olympus Mons on the planet Mars, is three times as high as Mount Everest.

If the oceans were drained away, the Earth's surface would look like a giant jigsaw puzzle. Most of the world's volcanoes can be found near or along the edges of these pieces.

You might be surprised to learn that there are volcanoes in Antarctica. Even beneath this frozen continent the Earth's core is still extremely hot. Australia seems to be the only place in the world where active volcanoes no longer exist. Perhaps you could try to find out why.

## GUESS WHAT?

When Krakatoa, an island near Java in Indonesia, blew apart in 1883 it left a crater nearly 300 meters (1,000 feet) deep in the ocean floor. Since then, small eruptions have built Anak Krakatoa ('child of Krakatoa') in part of the crater. A new volcano has formed.

## Under the sea

There are lots of volcanoes under the sea. Because the oceans are very, very deep not all volcanoes can be seen. Sometimes a volcano under the ocean keeps growing until it is tall enough to break the surface of the water. What might look like an island is often really a volcano. The Hawaiian islands were formed in this way.

Surtsey Island, in Iceland, rose out of the sea in 1963. By 1970, insects and birds were visiting the island.

# When do volcanoes erupt?

When red-hot magma spills from the Earth's crust, this is called an **eruption**. During an eruption, clouds of choking **ash** and poisonous gas can tumble down the mountain or be flung high into the air. It is certainly not safe to be near an erupting volcano.

Luckily, most volcanoes do not erupt all the time. The inside of the Earth is always moving and magma keeps bubbling up to the thin crust, but it is not usually strong enough to break through. If the magma keeps pushing at the surface where there is a weak spot in the Earth's crust, it will be able to burst through.

When a volcano erupts, magma emerges from the cone of the volcano as ash and lava.

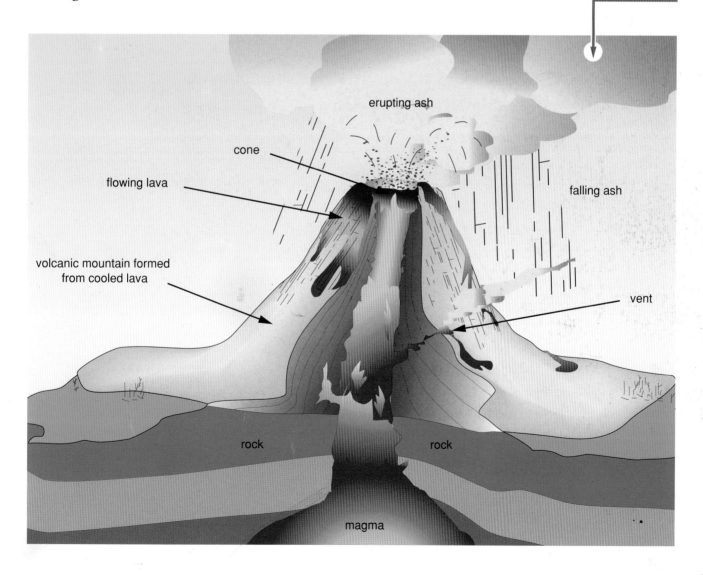

erupting ash

cone

flowing lava

falling ash

volcanic mountain formed from cooled lava

vent

rock

rock

magma

# Types of volcanoes

## Active

Volcanoes that are constantly bubbling and steaming with magma are called active volcanoes. Beware! This means they can erupt at any time.

White Island in New Zealand is an active volcano.

## Dormant

A volcano that has not erupted for some time is called a **dormant** volcano. A dormant volcano is only sleeping and can erupt suddenly without warning. Mount Vesuvius erupted after 600 years of silence.

Mount St Helens in North America had been asleep for more than 100 years when it erupted in 1980.

## Extinct

An extinct volcano is one that has not erupted for thousands of years. If an eruption is very violent it can empty all of the magma out of the cone. The walls of extinct volcanoes can collapse into the empty magma chamber, forming a huge crater called a **caldera**. Rainfall and melting snow can collect in a caldera, making a new lake.

Crater Lake in North America formed inside the caldera of an extinct volcano.

# How does a volcano erupt?

Volcanoes erupt in different ways. Some eruptions are like enormous explosions, with fountains of lava spurting from the crater; others are slower and more gentle. Sometimes, the shape of the volcano helps to control the lava flow.

## Types of eruptions

There are several different ways in which a volcano can erupt. A volcano may not always erupt the same way each time. Whichever way it erupts, death and **destruction** are often a problem.

### Hawaiian eruption

Magma is filled with bubbles of poisonous gas. If the magma is thin and runny the gas can escape from it. This makes the lava run more gently down the sides of the volcano. This is the most harmless type of eruption because people have more time to escape the lava flow.

Hawaiian eruptions are not explosive. This means that there is less poisonous gas and searing hot ash being flung into the air.

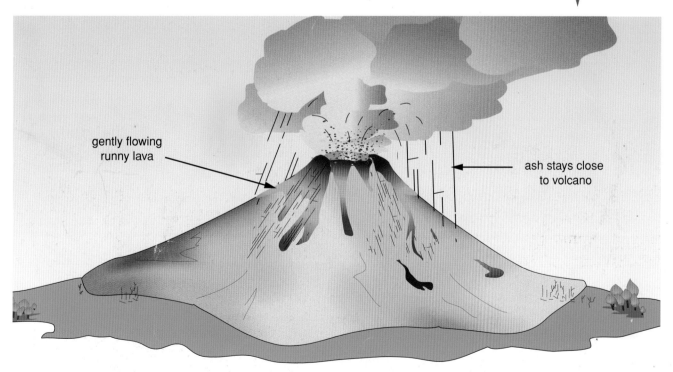

gently flowing runny lava

ash stays close to volcano

**Hawaiian eruption**

## Strombolian eruption

When the magma is thick and sticky like tar, gas is trapped inside. The gas keeps bubbling up until it explodes, splattering **molten** rock and ash everywhere. The lava is so thick it oozes out.

## Plinian eruption

A Plinian eruption is the most explosive eruption of all. In this kind of volcano, the magma is so thick and gluey that it clogs the crater. As it cools down it becomes a solid plug of rock. For hundreds of years the gas builds up behind this plug then … *BOOM*!

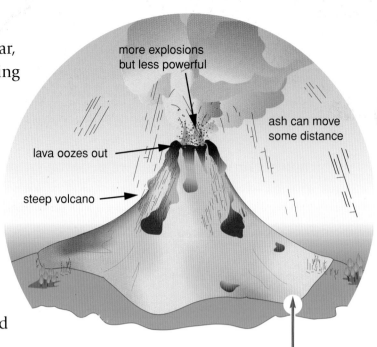

more explosions but less powerful

ash can move some distance

lava oozes out

steep volcano

**Strombolian eruption**

A Strombolian eruption has more explosions but they are not very powerful.

### Disaster Detective

There are other types of eruptions. Perhaps you can find out what they are called. Here is a clue: two of them are named after other famous volcanoes, and the other is named after the Roman god of fire.

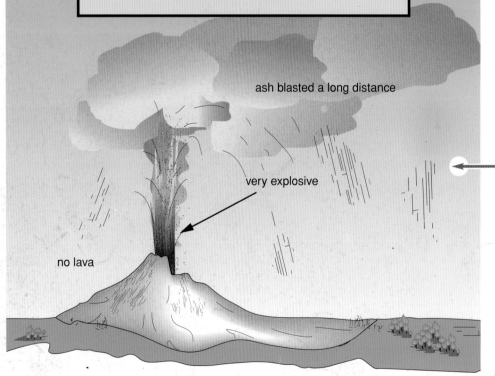

ash blasted a long distance

very explosive

no lava

**Plinian eruption**

The eruption of Mount St. Helens in May, 1980 is a good example of a violent Plinian eruption. Much of the mountain's peak was blasted away.

# What happens when a volcano erupts?

## Lava

When a volcano shoots lava into the air it can spurt upwards, sparking like a giant fireworks display. Lava can also come out as tiny stones called **lapilli**. Sometimes there are lumps of lava as big as a house! These are called **lava bombs**.

At first the lava is so hot that it sets fire to everything it touches. As it flows it is cooled by the air. Different kinds of lava will cool to form different kinds of rocks.

Burning lava has buried this house in Iceland.

## Aa

This kind of lava creeps along so slowly that it is hard to tell if it is moving. When it cools, it turns into rough, twisted lumps that can cut your feet if you step on them. This is **Aa** (pronounced *ahh!*) **lava**. It gets its name from the noise you make when its sharp edges slice into your feet.

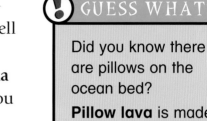
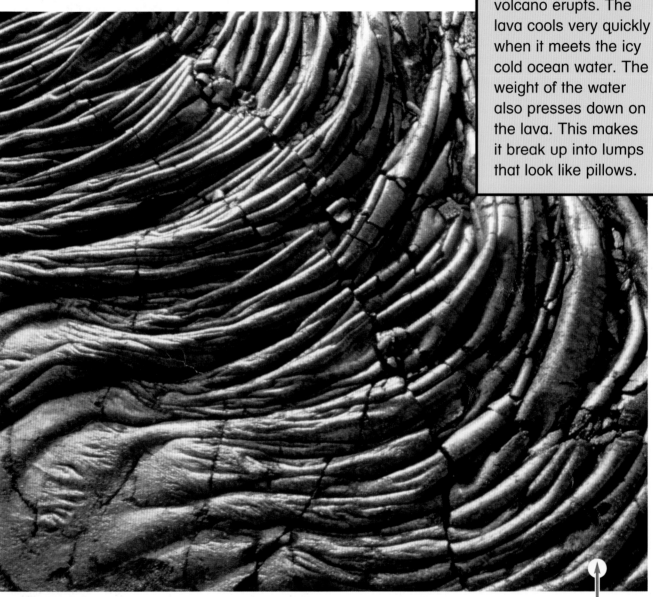

Pahoehoe lava. This strange lava looks a bit like a woven basket.

## Pahoehoe

Runny lava can flow very fast. When it cools it settles into smooth folds and looks like piles of rope. This is called **pahoehoe lava** (pronounced *pa hoy hoy*). It is Hawaiian for 'lava you can walk barefoot on'.

## Glowing clouds

Lava can also gush out as ash, dust and poisonous gas and can be seen as a great, glowing cloud. This scorching cloud shoots upwards into the atmosphere, blocking out the sunlight. There can be complete darkness for many days or weeks.

Crops and animals die because they cannot get enough sunlight to keep growing. Without the Sun's energy to warm the Earth, the weather becomes colder. Thousands of years ago, an ancient volcano blocked out the sunlight for so long the world went into a new ice age!

Glowing clouds can reach temperatures of 900 degrees Celsius (1,652 degrees Fahrenheit). They can burn, boil and melt everything they touch.

## Poisonous gas

The glowing cloud is a mixture of poisonous gas and **superheated** air. This air is so hot it can scorch the inside of your body when you breathe in. When a volcano erupted on the little island of Martinique, the hot, poisonous gases reached the town below so fast that people just breathed in and fell down dead. Only one person out of 28,000 survived.

## Ash

Ash settles on everything like a thick grey snow. It suffocates plants and animals and makes buildings collapse as it presses down on their roofs. Many people find it difficult to breathe. Aircraft can never fly near an erupting volcano: ash can clog the engines, making them stop. This can cause an aircraft to crash.

For weeks after Mount Pinatubo in the Philippines erupted, the ash fell like snow and people had to carry umbrellas to keep it from falling on them.

 Read All About It!

**Massive Volcanic Eruption Makes Monster Come to Life**

When Indonesia's Tambora volcano erupted in 1815, the ash cloud was so dense it upset the world's weather for a year. Mary Shelley went on a summer holiday to Switzerland in the same year, but the weather was too cold and wet for outside fun. Instead she stayed inside and wrote a story she was to become very famous for. It was called *Frankenstein*.

# What else can happen when a volcano erupts?

## Changing weather

A volcanic eruption can change the weather. An incredible amount of **intense** heat rushes high into the air, creating storm clouds and howling winds. When the winds blow the ash around at high speed, sparks and lightning can be seen streaking around the top of the volcano.

## Acid rain

Inside the clouds of gas from the volcano are chemicals that change into acid when they mix with water in the air. When it rains, the acid is washed back down to the earth where it destroys trees and plants. It falls into rivers and lakes, killing fish and insects and making the water unsafe to drink. Animals and birds that eat the plants and insects often die.

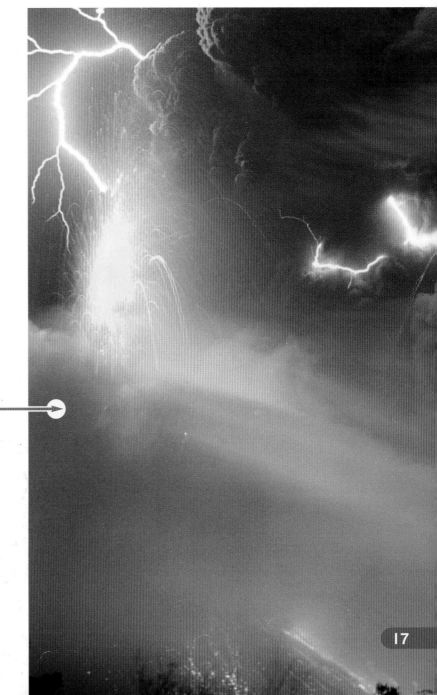

This lightning storm happened over the Pacaya volcano in Guatemala.

This flattened forest shows how powerful the Mount St Helens eruption was. A lahar killed two million forest animals.

## Lahars

When the storm clouds let go of all the rain inside them the rain mixes with the ash and soil on the slopes of the volcano. This mixture turns into thick, sludgy mud. There is so much of it that it soon begins to slide downhill. A **lahar** (pronounced *la ha*) can move very quickly, flattening forests and burying everything in its path.

## Giant ocean waves

When a volcano on land erupts violently it can shake the ground, causing earthquakes. When an underwater volcano erupts it can make the water at the bottom of the ocean surge upwards into a gigantic wave called a **tsunami**.

Tsunamis can kill more people than any other event that might happen during an eruption. If crops and farmland are covered with salt water, thousands of people can die of starvation and disease long after the wave has gone. Volcanoes can be dangerous in many different ways.

## Disappearing islands

Volcanoes can also make islands disappear. Krakatoa had been sleeping for over 200 years when it began to wake up. When Krakatoa finally erupted it blew the island in half! The explosion sent huge waves sweeping across nearby islands, drowning over 36,000 people as 300 towns and villages were washed away.

**Read All About It!**

**Krakatoa Erupts**
Gigantic waves circled the world for days after Krakatoa erupted, reaching as far as the USA. Twelve meter (40 feet) high waves carried the steamship *Berouw* deep into the Sumatran jungle.

# Other eruptions

## Hot springs and geysers

Near volcanoes there are underground rocks full of little holes that soak up water like sponges. When magma heats up the water inside these rocks, it can bubble up to the surface very gently to form a **hot spring**. In other places, water and steam may come squirting out at very high speed. This is called a **geyser**.

A geyser erupting in Rotorua, New Zealand. The gas escaping from the magma smells a lot like rotten eggs.

## Chimneys under the sea

It may sound strange, but there are chimneys under the sea. Hot springs on the ocean bed pump out water colored by the metals they contain. When these hot metals meet the very cold water they become hard and pile up to form pipes or chimneys. The metals that cloud the water are usually black and make the chimneys look as if they are smoking. That is why they are often called black smokers. If the metals are milky in color, the chimneys are called white smokers.

### Disaster Detective

The water near black smokers is always black and poisonous, yet tiny shrimp feed on the bacteria that swarm around these chimneys. A spot on the shrimps' backs can pinpoint the glow given out by the smokers. There are some other creatures that live happily in the dark depths alongside the smokers. See if you can find out what they are.

# Volcanoes can be useful

## Growing food

Not everything about volcanoes is bad. Soil that is made up of volcanic ash and lava is very rich in **minerals**. For plants, these minerals are important for healthy growth, and so growing near a volcano means that they are able to draw these minerals easily from the soil. Without eruptions, these minerals would stay locked inside the rocks deep beneath the ground.

Some people live near volcanoes because the soil is very fertile and good for agriculture. In Indonesia people use lava to help their crops grow.

## Power

Heat that comes from a volcano is an example of **geothermal energy**.

Special power stations can pump cold water down to the hot rocks beneath the ground. The rocks heat up the water, turning it into steam. The steam is then piped back up to the power station. Forcing the steam through pipes makes it strong enough to turn giant wheels called turbines. The turbines make electricity.

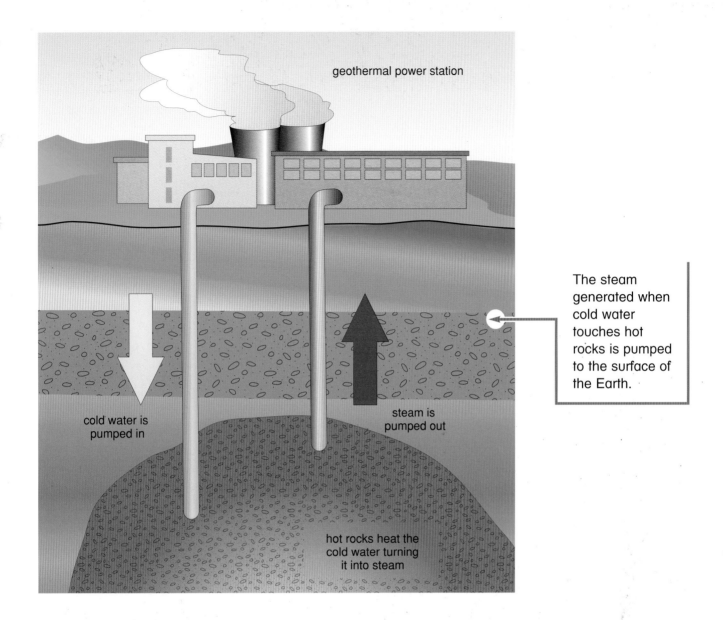

geothermal power station

The steam generated when cold water touches hot rocks is pumped to the surface of the Earth.

cold water is pumped in

steam is pumped out

hot rocks heat the cold water turning it into steam

## GUESS WHAT?

The people of Reykjavik, in Iceland, use the water from hot springs to heat their homes. This makes Reykjavik one of the most pollution-free cities in the world.

Most of our electricity comes from burning oil and coal. This damages the environment and can upset the weather. It is also a very dangerous job to bring the coal and oil from out of the ground. Geothermal power is cleaner and cheaper. However, not all countries have volcanic areas and so not everyone can use this type of energy. Only countries such as Japan, Iceland and New Zealand are able to use geothermal power.

Nature takes millions of years to make oil and coal by pressing the remains of dead animals and plants between layers of rock. We use so much electricity that we will soon run out of oil and coal to make it. An advantage of geothermal power is that the water can be recycled.

# Health

Many people believe that volcanic mud and the water from hot springs have special healing powers. Nobody has been able to prove it, but bathing in volcanic mud has been said to cure some diseases, relieve painful swollen limbs and help people to look younger.

A geothermal power station in Iceland. See the people bathing in the hot water? Some people believe the minerals might help to cure skin diseases.

### GUESS WHAT?

There are 4,000 hot springs in the Japanese town of Beppu. The giant Jungle Bath is nearly as big as four Olympic swimming pools. That makes it the biggest spa bath in the world.

## Diamonds and metals

Precious stones like diamonds are formed inside magma over many hundreds of years. Constant baking and the force of the rock layers pressing down makes a diamond so tough that it is almost **indestructible**. In South Africa, there is a diamond mine right in the crater of an extinct volcano.

Tin and copper are also made when certain kinds of rock minerals melt and mix together near a volcano.

These people are working in a diamond mine in South Africa.

### Disaster Detective

Take a look around your home. Can you find things that are made of tin or copper?

Some ornaments are made of copper. Copper is also thought to help relieve the pain of swollen joints and is made into bracelets for people with arthritis to wear. Hot water pipes are made of copper because the metal keeps the water hot for a lot longer than plastic pipes do. Tin should be easy to find—look in your pantry or refrigerator.

Perhaps you might like to find out if there are other metals that are made in the same way.

# Predicting volcanoes

The scientists who study volcanoes are called **volcanologists**. What volcanologists would really like to be able to do is work out when a volcano is going to erupt. This is called making a prediction. Why is it important to predict when a volcano is about to blow its top?

➤ People can be moved quickly to a safer place.

➤ There will be enough time to try and protect farms and homes from lava flows before everyone leaves the area.

The most dangerous thing about a volcano is that it can erupt without warning.

## Mount Vesuvius

Nearly 2,000 years ago Mount Vesuvius suddenly split open and an enormous glowing cloud tumbled out. Below the mountain, the town of Pompeii was buried so quickly that people could not escape. Two thousand people died almost instantly as a blast of scorching ash and lava four meters (12 feet) thick covered them.

Pompeii lay buried for nearly 1,600 years until it was rediscovered. The ash-covered bodies had rotted away, leaving their shape in the hardened lava. By filling these people-shaped holes with plaster, scientists were able to make models of the citizens and understand more about the daily life of this **ancient** town.

A cast of one of the victims of the eruption of Mount Vesuvius.

Pumice stone is hardened lava and you can use it to remove hard skin from your feet. If you have some at home, find out what happens when pumice stone is placed in water. It floats!

Pumice is covered with tiny holes from burst gas bubbles. This makes pumice so light that it can float on top of water.

## Finding out about volcanoes is a dangerous job

Volcanologists need to get very close to a volcano to take its temperature and collect samples of rock and gas. Rocks and gases found near the volcano will give them clues as to what is happening beneath the ground.

By placing a long rod into the crater and swirling it around, volcanologists collect lava in the same way that cotton candy gathers around its wooden stick.

Look at the suit the volcanologist is wearing. The head covering stops the poisonous gas from getting into the lungs and eyes.

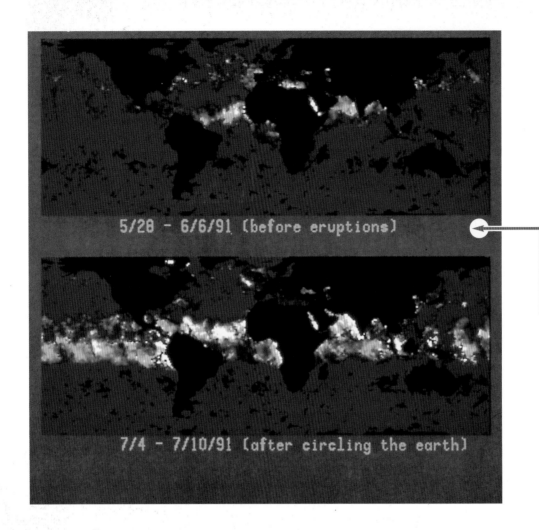

5/28 - 6/6/91 (before eruptions)

7/4 - 7/10/91 (after circling the earth)

A satellite tracked the ash and gas from the eruption of Mount Pinatubo in the Philippines. The ash caused many problems for aircraft.

## Satellites

A satellite is a spacecraft that spins around the Earth, sending back signals that can be changed into pictures on a special screen. Satellites also have measuring instruments that can record temperatures in different parts of the world.

When magma rises, it brings heat from within the Earth. This makes the volcano become hotter. From space, a satellite can measure even small changes in a volcano's temperature.

Knowing when a volcano is about to erupt is very helpful. However, volcanologists still cannot predict what the size or effects of that eruption will be.

# Protection from volcanoes

Nobody can stop a volcano from erupting. It is probably not very wise to try! Like everything in nature, volcanoes have a special job to do. When magma rises to the surface, it brings with it heat from the center of the Earth. Pushing this heat out from the ground helps to stop the Earth's core from getting too hot.

The only way to be safe during an eruption is to be as far away as possible. Moving people to safety is called an evacuation. Sometimes people do not want to leave. They stay behind and try very hard to stop lava and ash from ruining their crops by building ditches or dams around their homes and farms. If a skin forms on the lava, holes can be punched in it, making the lava leak out and run in a different direction.

Explosives are used to dig deep trenches so that lava flows can be guided around farms and villages.

## Heimaey

In 1973, on the Icelandic island of Heimaey, an enormous crack suddenly appeared in the ground behind the town. Lava and ash blasted up into the sky. Sea water was pumped from the nearby beach onto the eruption to cool the lava before it could set fire to the town. Ash was shovelled from the roofs before it piled up and collapsed homes. Much of the town was saved from destruction because the people stayed.

## Shelters

In countries like Japan, where lots of people share the land with volcanoes, there is not always enough time to evacuate everyone before an eruption. Special shelters have been built to protect everyone from showers of lava bombs. People practice preparing for this emergency in the same way as you practice fire drills at work and school.

**GUESS WHAT?**

Volcanoes are named after Vulcan, the Roman god of fire and metalwork. The ancient Romans believed that Vulcan lived deep inside the Earth, where he kept a great furnace burning.

Living near an active volcano means taking special precautions.

# After a volcano erupts

The lava from a volcanic eruption will eventually cool into rock. If the lava pours onto the beach it can make a new coastline so that maps have to be changed. This happened on the island of Heimaey.

> Can you imagine how the coastline of Heimaey changed after the volcanic eruption?

Volcanoes can erupt without warning, so homes can suddenly be buried under lava, ash or a lahar. If the volcano is under water, buildings may be swept away by a tsunami. It is not unusual for whole towns or villages to need rebuilding after an eruption.

Some people become so afraid they decide to move to a safer place. Developing countries, like Indonesia or the Philippines, rely on developed countries like Australia and the USA to help them recover from such terrible destruction. If the volcanic soil helps strong, healthy crops to grow, most of these people cannot afford to leave. The land may be the only way they can feed their families.

> **GUESS WHAT?**
>
> The crack that suddenly opened on Heimaey almost split the island in two. It did not close until nearly five months later.

# Record-breaking volcanoes

## The loudest eruption in the world

**Krakatoa**

The eruption of this volcanic island in Indonesia was heard nearly 5,000 kilometers (3,000 miles) away.

## The most eruptions in one day

**Mayon volcano**

The Mayon volcano in the Philippines erupted 26 times on August 13, 1984.

## The deadliest volcano

**Tambora**

It is thought that 92,000 people died in Indonesia in 1815 when this eruption happened. Huge ash falls buried many of them. Others died later from starvation because crops and farmland were smothered.

## The tallest geyser

**Steamboat geyser**

Water and steam spurting from the Steamboat geyser in the USA reaches a height of 115 meters (125 yards). The Waimangu geyser in New Zealand used to shoot over 460 meters (over 500 yards), but it has not erupted for nearly 100 years.

## The most active volcano

**Kilauea**

This Hawaiian volcano has been erupting continuously since 1983.

## The longest lava flow

**The Roza flow**

This happened in North America about 15 million years ago! The flow stretched for 300 kilometers (190 miles).

# Glossary

| | |
|---|---|
| **Aa lava** | A type of sharp-edged lava. |
| **ancient** | Very, very old or long ago. |
| **ash** | Tiny pieces of magma thrown from a volcano. |
| **caldera** | A large volcanic crater left when a magma chamber is emptied. |
| **cone** | The top part of a volcano. |
| **crust** | The thin layer of rock on the surface of the Earth. |
| **destruction** | When something is destroyed. |
| **dormant** | Has not erupted for some time. |
| **eruption** | When magma flows through holes in the Earth's crust. |
| **geothermal energy** | Energy from the hot rocks below the Earth's surface. |
| **geyser** | A hot spring that shoots hot water and steam into the air. |
| **hot spring** | A gentle eruption of hot water from beneath the ground. |
| **indestructible** | Unable to be destroyed. |
| **intense** | Extremely hot or strong. |
| **lahar** | A mudslide of water, ash and soil. |
| **lapilli** | Tiny pebbles of magma. |
| **lava** | Liquid magma that flows from a volcano and cools to become solid rock. |
| **lava bombs** | Very large lumps of magma thrown from a volcano. |
| **magma** | Rock that has become so hot it has melted. |
| **minerals** | Metals formed inside underground rocks. |
| **molten** | Rock or metal that has been heated until it becomes a thick, sticky liquid. |
| **pahoehoe lava** | A type of lava that cools to become smooth rock. |
| **pillow lava** | A type of lava flowing from undersea volcanoes and shaped by the cold ocean water. |
| **superheated** | When something is heated to an extremely high temperature. |
| **tsunami** | A giant ocean wave started by an undersea eruption. |
| **volcanologist** | A scientist who studies volcanoes. |

# Index

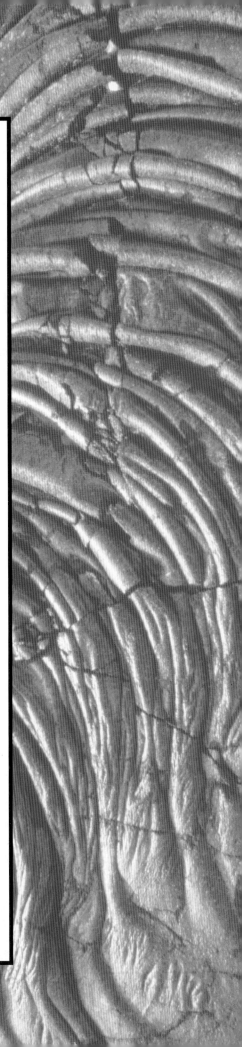